Hair Raisin' Funds
Murder Mystery Plays

Incident at the Road Kill Café, Rawhide, The Castlemeyer Fortune

By

Suzann Carr

ISBN: 1-4033-8573-4 (e-book)
ISBN: 1-4033-8574-2 (Paperback)

Library of Congress Control Number: 2002095171

This book is printed on acid free paper.

Printed in the United States of America
Bloomington, IN

1stBooks – rev. 10/25/02

Hair Raisin' Funds
Presents...

Hair Raisin' Funds
Murder Mystery Plays

All the plays are "G" rated and
An excellent way to raise funds

Let's put the _Fun_ back into your _Fun_draising!

Incident at the Road Kill Café'

Written by:
Suzann Carr

Suzann Carr

© The Incident at the Road Kill Café

Fern Bailey – Now this lady knows how to wait tables. Rumor has it that she has a great recipe for Armadillo stew. She's honest and that means her and Daley don't have too much in common.

Beau Stanley – He is sweet on Fern. But she said kissing Beau is like kissing her brother!

Daley Bread – Daley is the manager of the Road Kill Café. He is mean and stingy. Fern has to keep an eye on her tips.

Samuel Bacon – Sam is the Deputy of Greenbow. The Sheriff quit and he is trying to keep the town in line. He needs help running the town, soon!

Cindy Lou – Cindy Lou is the town gossip. She owns the local beauty shop next to the Road Kill Café. It's called the Hair and Polish Beauty Shop. She is single. When you meet her you **will** know why!

Darren Finely – Darren is the town's most eligible bachelor. Darren can't seem to find his place in life. Maybe he should go into politics.

Mayor Bradley – He is Cindy Lou's Daddy. He wants grandchildren <u>so</u> bad. He has about given up on Cindy Lou. Even he can't be in the same room with her for more than five minutes.

Lavana Webb – Lavana does the manicures at the Hair and Polish beauty shop. She's new in town. Only been in Greenbow 19 years.

Shad Watson – Shad can't seem to stay out of trouble. He sure knows his way around. The swamp I mean.

Uncle Elmer and the Schoolteacher – Missing in action! Read on and find out why!

Narrator – He narrates!

Welcome to Greenbow

Sit down and stay a spell,
Fern will wait on you and keep you well.

The Mayor might wave as you pass by,
While listening to Cindy Lou will make you cry.

Daley only wants your tourist dollars,
While the Deputy drags Darren by the collar.

Lavana will touch your heart,
When Shad just wants to kiss and then part.

Beware the friendship will soon end,
When someone is murdered the mystery begins!

This play read out loud with no stops or breaks was 52 minutes long.

Scene I

This scene takes place at the Road Kill Café. Fern is busy rushing around.

Beau – Hey Fern, can you come and take my order? I've got to get back to the garage.

Fern – I'll be with you as soon as I can. Keep your shirt on!

Beau – I hope they haven't run out of Fern's stew.

*There's a sign that has the **"Daily Specials." Armadillo stew, Ferns recipe.***

Fern – What'll it be Beau?

Beau – How bout my house about eight o'clock?

Fern – I'm old enough to be your, uh, your..older sister. You want the "Special?"

Beau – Yea that'll do. Thanks.

Fern puts the pencil back behind her ear and runs to the back to turn her order in. Beau hears two of the customers talking about an old so-called murder that never got solved.

Beau – Hey, what are y'all talkin about?

Darren – I was just tellin Lavona about that murder that happened back twenty some odd years ago.

Lavana – I moved here not long after and nobody wanted to talk about it. How come?

Beau – I'll tell ya how come. Because it was the Mayor's Uncle who was involved with the whole mess. His name was Elmer Bradley. He was a very strange man.

Lavana – Is that where Cindy Lou gets her weirdness? From her Uncle. That would make sense.

Darren – No, Cindy Lou *never* shuts up. Old man Bradley never said too much. I'll tell you all about it. We had a new schoolteacher come to town that summer. She was in her fifties and we were told that she could handle any situation. She came highly recommended from the school board down in Hidden Valley. So, after she had worked a few weeks at the old school house to get it set up the way she wanted, old man Bradley started comin around and talkin to her. We were surprised. He never spoke to anyone but his nephew, the Mayor. When the teacher finally had the finishing touches on her little schoolhouse, she came by here to try some of Fern's stew. Fern has become quite famous because of her stew. Not five minutes after the teacher had sat down, in walks old man Bradley. He never ate out. In fact, we never saw him buy any food at the dry good store either. He went up to the teacher and asked her on a date. The café was so quiet; you could hear your own heart beat. The teacher looked up at old man Bradley and said that she was sorry, she couldn't get involved because she was married to her job and that was teaching. Old man Bradley began to shake. I guess he felt humiliated. He was carrying his shotgun, like he always did and he aimed it at the teacher and made her leave with him. None of us knew what to do. So we followed them. You see, the old man lived down in the Youkachokea swamp. If you tried to go down there, you may never find your way out. We heard the hooty owls a hooten and the peepers a peepin and we got the heck out of there. We lost sight of them and have never seen either one of them since. Rumor has it that they are both dead and they haunt the swamp where they died. I don't know what to think.

Lavona – Wow, what a story, Darren. You saw all that?

Darren – Yep, me and half the town of Greenbow.

Beau – Since that day the rumors have flown around this town like crazy. I bet there have been about a million sightings of the schoolteacher and old man Bradley.

Lavona – Do you think any of them are true?

Darren – Well, something happened to them. I would bet my bottom dollar that the old man tortured the teacher.

Beau – You don't know that for a fact. Don't go starting any more rumors, Darren.

Lavana – It's been real but I've got to get back to the beauty shop. So when did that incident happen anyways?

Beau – It was on a Friday the 13th. (*Sound Effect of cast*) Right before school was to start that semester.

Darren – Today's the 13th-(*sound effect*)

Lavana – You two are just messin' with me. It can't be today can it?

Beau – Well I'll be darn, today is the twentieth anniversary of the Youkachokea Swamp incident.

Lavana – That's kinda creepy. Hey Darren, will you walk me to the Beauty shop?

Darren – Sure thing. The thought of being dragged into the swamp gives me the creeps too.

Beau – You two worry too much. That was a long time ago. Life is too short to stick our noses in somebody else's mess.

Darren – See ya later, Beau.

Lavana – Be sure and come by and get your hair cut later, Beau. You need a trim.

Beau – Okay, I will. Bye, you two.

Lavana and Darren leave and Fern brings Beau his food. The "special."

Fern – What were the three of you talking about for so long?

Beau – Darren was tellin' Lavana about the Youkachokea swamp incident.

Fern – Oh no, here we go again. I'm beginning to wonder if that really happened.

Beau – Fern, you *were* there. You have lied about your age so much that I think that you are beginning to believe yourself!

Fern – You could be right about that. Now don't you go tellin' anybody about my age. I'll skin you alive. Ya hear?

Beau – I've seen you skin an armadillo so I won't say a word. You have nothing to concern yourself with. You can trust me, Fern.

Fern – Just hearing you talk like that gives me the willies. I'd better get back to the customers. See ya later.

Beau – Yeah, thanks for the grub, it's mighty tasty. (*talking to himself*) Boy, that woman can cook. She ain't bad lookin', (*taking to the audience*) you know, for her age and all.

Daley comes in to check on Fern.

Daley – Fern, what were those three talkin about? I couldn't make it out where I was standin'.

Fern – You ought to be ashamed of yourself. (*Slaps Daley on the arm.*) Oh well, I'll tell ya anyway. Darren was tellin' Lavana about the Youkachokea swamp incident that happened twenty years ago today!

Daley – Is that right! I'll be. I can turn that anniversary into a money makin' event.

Fern – Now you just wait a minute, Daley. You can't make money at someone else's expense. It just isn't right.

Daley – Fern, are you forgettin that we live in a free country? It ain't illegal for me to cash in on something that happened right here in this cafe twenty years ago. I have some ideas. I'd better go, I'm burnin' daylight, Fern. Oh, and stick around after your shift. I might need some help with my plannin' and all. See ya, wouldn't want to be ya! Ha Ha Ha.

Daley runs off laughing and mumbling to him self like any nut would. He makes a big banner and returns to put it up. He needs help. The banner reads, **"20th Anniversary of the Youkachokea Swamp Incident", Buy one daily special and get the second one half price!** *No one said that Daley was smart.*

Daley – Fern, get over here. I need your assistance. What do you think about this here banner?

Fern – (*slowly reads banner*) I can't believe you did it! This is in poor taste. Nobody is going to fall for this!

Daley – (*he takes off his jacket and he has a T-shirt that says "20th Youkachokea Swamp Anniversary" 1981-2001. Fern is almost speechless.*)
So Fern, what do think about my T-shirt?

Fern – I (*stutters*) I, I can't believe you would have this printed up. This is, well, it is just an out right disgrace! Why do I work here?

Daley – Cause you're poor and you don't have a choice. Even I can figure that one out, Fern. Well, I've got to run. I'm selling my T-shirts at a stand outside. I bet I can get $20.00 a piece!

Fern – (*yelling*) I hope you choke on all that money, Daley.

Daley – Oh I get it, Youka**choke**ka Swamp, real funny, Fern. Gotta go. Bye!

Fern – That man needs serious help. It's probably too late for him!

Cindy Lou enters the café with her Daddy, Mayor Bradley.

Mayor – I can't believe that Daley is having a 20th anniversary special. Is he forgetting who the incident was all about?

Cindy Lou – Daddy you know the type of people that live in this silly little town. No manners, no taste, no class…

As Cindy Lou is talking, basically to herself, her Daddy calls Fern over to the table and Cindy walks around the audience and continues to share her knowledge with them.

Mayor – (*talking over his daughter*) Fern could you help me out here? What's all of this 20th anniversary mess?

Cindy Lou is still talking to herself – No money to speak of. No one is good lookin' except for Darren and Sam of course, then there's no excitement, no one to go to lunch with…no movie theater, no massage parlors, no sushi bar…no McDonald's..no payless shoe store, no place to bungee jump, no hat store…No wedding dress store, no Victoria Secrets, no Wal –Mart, no K-Mart,

Fern – I'm so sorry Mayor. I tried to talk some sense into Daley. Of course you know how that went. All he sees is dollar signs.

Mayor – This is embarrassing enough without him reminding the town about the Youkachokeka Swamp incident. You know Daley better than any of us. What do you think we should do Fern?

Fern – If I were you Mayor, I would go outside and buy up all of Daleys T-shirts. I know that he would make money out of it, but very few people would know about the incident.

About that time a couple of people walk in with the 20th anniversary T-shirts on.

Mayor – It appears that I may be too late in saving the family name.

Cindy Lou is still talking to herself about what Greenbow in lacking. Daley comes in and joins the Mayor at his table.

Daley – Well, Well, Well, look what we have here. I did not expect to see you here today Mayor. Hi Cindy Lou.

Cindy Lou just waves off Daley and keeps talking to herself.

Mayor – What in tarnation are you doing to my family name Daley?

Daley – I'm just turning a profit so I can retire someday in the lifestyle that I've become accustom to living! *(Daley sticks his chest out and pulls us his pants)*

Fern – *(slaps Daley in the stomach)* Stop acting like a rooster in a hen house. You're being just plain mean. I'll tell you what, if you don't stop selling those T-shirts and you also have to take down that banner. *(points to banner)* I will never make another pot of armadillo stew again.
The entire cafe gasps and even Cindy Lou stops chattering.

Daley – Fern, *(speaking slowly)* do you mean what you are saying?

11

Fern – I'm afraid so Daley. You know that it is not right to take advantage of a bad situation and make money off of it. You stop or no more armadillo stew.

Daley – It appears that you have left me no choice. I will take down my banner and stop selling T-shirts.

The whole restaurant cheers and claps.

Daley – Oh all of you people be quiet. I'm about out of T-shirts anyways. So there! (*sticks his tongue out at his own customers*)

Daley storms out of the café and Cindy Lou is still quiet.

Mayor – Fern I owe you one. That was a big chance that you took.

Fern – Don't worry about a thing. He wouldn't have agreed if he hadn't sold most of his T-shirts anyway. Besides he eats more of my stew than anyone else! (*Looks over at Cindy Lou.*) Cindy Lou are you feelin okay? I haven't heard a peep out of you in nearly three maybe four minutes.

Cindy Lou – I was just taken aback Fern.(*puts the back of her hand to her forehead*) I've been eating your stew since I was a toddler. You just found a way to keep me quiet, I guess.

Mayor – Remember that Fern, we may need to threaten her again sometime! (*The Mayor & Fern high-5 each other*) We've gotta get going. Holler at me if Daley starts up again. I'll be in my office. Cindy Lou has to get back to the beauty shop.

Fern – No problem Mayor. See ya later Cindy Lou.

Cindy Lou – Drop by later and I'll paint your nails for ya Fern. Be sure and bring me some armadillo stew when you stop by.

The Mayor and Cindy Lou leave the Café. Samuel the Deputy runs into the Mayor going out of the café.

Samuel – Hey there Mayor. What's all the commotion outside?

Mayor – Where in the world have you been? Daley was celebrating the 20th anniversary of the Youkachokeka Swamp incident. He was turning a profit from it too!

Samuel – Now he sure has some nerve. Has it been twenty years already? I was just a kid when that happened. I remember it like it was yesterday. We don't have too many days like that happen here in Greenbow.

Mayor – Are you finished reminiscing? I want you to keep an eye on Daley. He said that he wasn't going to sell any more souvenirs but I want to make sure.

Samuel – No problem Mayor. I'll just sit a spell and have some of Fern's stew.

Mayor – You do that. I'll be in touch Samuel. Stay right here! (*points as he speaks*)

Samuel – No need to worry. I've got everything under control Mayor.

The Mayor exits and Fern brings Samuel his stew. He is very predictable. Shad enters the café and tries to exit when he sees the Deputy.

Samuel – Hey wait a minute Shad. Where ya headed? I need to talk to ya.

Shad – (*under his breath*) Oh great.

Samuel – Sit down and have some lunch on me.

Shad – Did I hear you correctly Deputy? On you?

13

Samuel – Sure you did. Can't I buy an **old** friend lunch?

Shad – An **old** friend? I got the feeling a long time ago that you didn't like me Samuel. Why the sudden change?

Samuel – Simple, I need your help.

*Samuel motions to Fern to bring more stew for his **friend**.*

Shad – At least you're honest. That's more than I can say for most of this town. What help do you need?

Samuel - You know what day it is?

Shad – Yea I know. I got my 20th anniversary T-shirt from Daley earlier. I plan on wearing it next time Mayor Bradley is up for re-election. I may just run against him.

Samuel – I wouldn't be surprised. But I need you to go down to the swamp with me to see if we can find anything related to the incident.

Shad – Samuel, it's been twenty years. What are we going to find? Two skeletons? Ha Ha! Besides, I might get turned around. You know it's a full moon tonight. Strange things happen on a full moon Samuel.

Samuel – Don't go and give me the willies. I hate the swamp. I should have moved a long time ago.

Shad – Why are you still here? The Mayor wants to replace you and you don't make much money.

Samuel – Thanks for the pep talk. Let's just say I have my eyes on a pretty little lady.

Shad – In Greenbow? Did someone move to town and I wasn't told?

Samuel – Real funny Shad. Let's get back to business. I know that you know the swamp. You're the only one that does. Now how come you don't want to take me down there?

Shad – It's not a walk in the park. I used to go there when I would get into trouble dating someone who's Daddy didn't want me around. Of course I was a lot younger. It's a good place to hide.

Samuel – We need to put to rest this Youkachokeka Swamp incident. If we find some kind of evidence as to what happened to the Teacher and Elmer then the Mayor and all of us can go on with our lives.

Shad – I know you Samuel. There's more to this than you're tellin me. I'll take you down there but you won't like it. Of course we may find some road kill on the way for Fern. Maybe she would like some fresh alligator meat?

Samuel – I believe she can cook anything. Even skunk!

Shad – I draw the line on that one.

Samuel – Let's go and get this over with. Before I chicken out.

Shad – Okay, don't forget your gun. I'm sure that you'll need it.

Shad and Samuel leave the café. Daley sees them leave and puts his banner back up. He takes off his jacket and underneath he has on his 20ᵗʰ anniversary T-shirt. Fern is busy working to notice what Daley is up to.

Lavana walks in the café.

Lavana – Hey Fern, when do you get off? You promised to help me finish my dress I'm makin'.

Fern – This place is finally starting to slow down. It shouldn't be but just a few minutes. *(Looks over at Daley)*Hey Daley, you'd better take down that banner. I'm starting to forget my recipe for the stew!

Daley – **Okay**! *(To the audience)*She's mean, mean, mean. I can't believe I put up with this.

Lavana – I saw Samuel and Shad head down towards the swamp. Do you know what their up to?

Fern – The swamp? And what are those two doing together? It sure seems fishy to me Lavana.

Lavana – Yea, me too. Let's get goin'. Daley can close up. Maybe workin' will keep him out of trouble.

Fern – I doubt that. Let's go.

Fern hands Daley her apron and her and Lavana leave the café. The Mayor peeks his head in and checks on Daley.

Mayor – *(yells across the café and startles Daley)* Hey Daley, I hear you've been breaking your promises.

Daley – Leave me alone. The workdays over. No body cares about your precious family name anyway.

Mayor – See ya in church Sunday Daley.

Daley – Okay, see ya Sunday Mayor. What's the sermon about anyway?

Mayor – Confession is good for the soul and lying and money changing in the temple.

Daley – I may not be well Sunday, I'll get back to ya Mayor.
Mayor is laughing and shaking his head as he goes out the door.

Scene II

Darren runs into the Mayor outside of the Road Kill Café.

Mayor – Where are you headed Darren?

Darren – I've got a date Mayor.

Mayor – Anyone I know?

Darren – Chances are in a town this size, you sure do!

Mayor – I haven't seen Samuel lately. Do you know where he's run off to?

Darren – Haven't a clue Mayor.

Mayor – Now you wouldn't lie to me would you Darren?

Darren – Not unless it was absolutely necessary sir.

Mayor – I'm not surprised. Can you at least give me a hint where Samuel has run off to?

Darren – It's in a ten-mile radius. That's all I can tell you.

Mayor – **Everything** is in a ten-mile radius Darren. I need just one more hint.

Darren – Okay, he's not alone.

Mayor – Not alone huh. Did he have a date? That would be more exciting than the Youkachokeka Swamp incident!

Darren – Ha Ha Mayor. You said one more hint and I gave it to you. I need to go now.

Mayor – Thanks anyway. Stay out of trouble, it's a full moon you know and a Friday the 13th.

Darren – I hate Friday the 13ths. They give me the creeps.

Mayor – Me too. I think I'll check on Cindy Lou and head on home. See ya later Darren.

Darren – See ya Mayor.

The Mayor is about to head over to the Beauty Salon and runs into Cindy Lou.

Cindy Lou – Hi Daddy. Where are you headed?

Mayor – I was on my way to your shop, thought I would make sure that you have a safe trip home.

The Mayor and Cindy Lou walk out together as Cindy Lou starts talking to herself again.

Cindy Lou – Oh yea, it's a full moon. It would be so nice to have a date and go down by the water and watch it come up and smooch and make wedding plans and talk about having babies and maybe a puppy…

Mayor – You're losing me again Cindy Lou. We need to get going. It's getting late.

Scene III

Narrator: Daley is locking up the café. The Mayor is walking Cindy Lou home. Darren is with Fern and Lavana while they put the finishing touches on Lavana's new dress. It's for church of course. Darren's date turned out to be hanging out with old friends. The Mayor doesn't need to know everything. All of a sudden there is a Hair Raising Scream from the Youkachokeka Swamp. It's hard to tell if it's a man or woman that screamed. All of a sudden Samuel and Shad come running down the main street. Their clothes are filthy and torn. They look like they've been in a fight with an alligator. That's a possibility.

Fern – Where have you two been? My goodness just look at you. Are you okay?

Samuel – You tell her Shad. I think I just wet my pants.

Shad – I'm not sure where to start Fern. It's been a long day.

Lavana – I saw you two headed to the swamp this afternoon. Why would you go down there?

Shad – It wasn't my idea. It was his. I was just his guide.

Fern – You know your way around the swamp Shad?

Shad – Um, well maybe.

Mayor – Maybe! Why didn't you ever tell me?

Shad – I kind of used the swamp to hide out when I would get into trouble when I was young and I just never told anyone.

Cindy Lou – Why would anyone want to go down there anyways?

Samuel – Because I thought that Shad could help this town put the swamp incident behind them. If he could help me find some clue that the Schoolteacher and Elmer were alive or dead or whatever!

Mayor – That's mighty noble of you Samuel. I'm impressed with your courage. No one else in the last twenty years has tried to solve that case.

Samuel – I can't say that we solved it. But we certainly know that someone was down there. We saw somebody. We just couldn't tell if it was a man or woman.

Mayor – You saw someone?

Daley – This is great. I can make a fortune on this. What else did you see?

Everyone in unison say's "Shut up Daley."

Shad – I had us about a half mile down and we both saw a shadow of some kind. It was a human but the trees are so thick it's hard to make out things.

Samuel – I had my gun. But I didn't want to shoot at someone that wasn't harming us.

Shad – Yea, I think they meant to scare us off.

Samuel – They did a good job too! (*pulls at his "wet" pants*)

Daley – I bet I know who that was. It was **Elvis**! He's decided to retire in Greenbow. Think of the possibilities.

Everyone in unison say's "Shut up Daley!" A couple of the people slap him on top of the head.

Mayor – What we need to do is send you two back down there.

Shad – I don't think so. I've lost about twenty years off of my life tonight. That's enough for one day.

Samuel – He's right Mayor. You don't realize just how eerie it is down there.

Daley – Don't forget what the date is now y'all. Friday the 13th. (*He makes scary noises and laughs loudly*)

Mayor – We don't need any *help* from you Daley. What do you say boys. I'll give you anything you want.

Samuel – Anything?

Mayor – You heard me right Samuel. What is it that will get you back down in the swamp?

Samuel whispers something in the Mayors ear.

Mayor – You have got to be kidding? (*Samuel shakes his head up and down*) I'm pretty sure I can grant that wish Samuel. But you have really surprised me. Now are you sure that's what you want? (*Samuel shakes his head up and down again*). Okay then.

Fern – What does he want anyway?

Mayor – If he makes it out alive, you'll all find out.

Everyone starts talking at once.

Shad – Now hold on everyone. I'm the one who knows how to get around down there. I can't think of anything worth making me go back.

Lavana – What if the Mayor gave you his horse?

Shad – Have you seen his horse? No teeth.

21

Fern – What about his belt buckle collection?

Shad – I rather have his belly button lent than that old stuff.

Darren – What about his office?

Shad – I think we may have something here! I always wanted to be Mayor. Okay if you will let me be the Mayor for 24 hours, I'll go back down to the swamp.

Mayor – I know this town will never survive you in charge. If you stay within the town's by-laws it's a deal.

Darren – Hot Dog, we're gonna have a blast. You had better make it out of that Swamp Shad. Good luck, you're gonna need it. Oh, I can't wait to change a few of these useless laws in this one horse town. The fun we're gonna have!

Shad – Gee Darren what are friends for? I don't think that I'll need your help but thanks for thinking of yourself. We had better get going Samuel.

Scene IV

Shad and Samuel head out one more time to Youkachokeka Swamp to solve the twenty-year-old mystery. The gang cheers them on as they disappear down the road.

Fern – Mayor, I think that you are being a little on the selfish side. If something happens to Samuel or Shad it will be on your head.

Mayor – They're grown men. You don't need to worry about them.

Darren – So Mayor, what is it that Samuel requested from you?

Mayor – I promised not to say anything until they get back. Boy will you all be surprised!

Narrator: Things did not go as planned. It's been two days and no sign of Samuel and Shad. The town is starting to panic. Especially the Mayor. Even Cindy Lou has been real quiet. Daley is in a panic. His business is slow and Fern won't cook a dead thing. I mean a darn thing. Darren has been trying to figure out what laws to change when **he** and Shad are Mayor for the day. Nothing is the same in Greenbow. Then on the third day…

Darren runs into the café where everyone is moping around.

Darren – Mayor, Mayor it's them. I see them coming up the road and they're not alone. They've got two people with them.

Everyone starts talking at once. In walks Samuel and Shad and two strangers.

Samuel – Everyone needs to calm down. Shad and I have finally solved the Youkachokeka Swamp Mystery.

Mayor – These two sure look familiar. Do we know them?

Samuel - You used to. This here is the Schoolteacher and of course you remember Uncle Elmer?

Cindy Lou – I'll be darn Daddy. Can you believe your eyes?
Mayor – How in tarnation did you find them? I've got to sit down. (*The Mayor sits and starts to fan himself*)

Shad – It wasn't easy. At first we thought we were being chased by ghosts. Those two sure are tricky. We would take turns sleeping so the other one could keep watch. After the first day we had seen signs where people had walked. We would pick up a good trail and then just like that (*snaps his fingers*) it would disappear.

Fern – Did you two ever get lost?

Samuel – As long as Shad knew where this certain spot was, we were okay. Everyday we would start at that spot and finish with it. But last night was just plain wild.

Daley – I think I hear my business pickin up.

Unison – " Be quiet Daley!"

Shad – We thought we knew about the location of where the "ghost" was living. We had hiked about four miles into the swamp. I had a small boat that we could paddle around in. When we got way down into a part of the swamp I had never seen, we heard music.

Samuel – It was real festive like. At first I thought I was going crazy. As we got closer to the music that's when we saw Uncle Elmer and the Schoolteacher. They have a small resort way back in there where rich people go to be in isolation and have mud baths and stuff. They named it the Youkachokeka Spa and Resort. Can you believe that?

Shad – We had to sit and watch for hours waiting for those two to be alone. Then when the time was right, we kidnapped them, tided them up and put them in the boat. I figured they owed this whole town an explanation.

Mayor – That's the most incredible story I have ever heard. I can't wait to hear what those two have to say.

Samuel – I've got to tell you Mayor. They have a real nice place back there. You can get to it by a back road from the other side. It's covered by trees and brush and almost impossible to find the road. They did a good job making them selves not exist.

Mayor – Uncle Elmer, you have some explaining to do!

Uncle Elmer – Honey, you go first. You know how shy I am.

Schoolteacher – I guess I should start the day that Sweetkins here dragged me out of this café. (*Looking around the café.*) This place hasn't changed one bit. Elmer and I had been seeing each other at the schoolhouse and we had become, well close. The day that he came in here and asked me for a date was the day I had got a bit upset with him because he was supposed to meet me at the school. When he asked me for a date I told him no, to get back at him of course. I knew it took a lot of nerve for him to ask me in a public place. He got upset and took me down to the swamp. We of course made up. We had got married the day after we left Greenbow. We went up to Rawhide and found a preacher to marry us. Not long after that we started our own business. We just celebrated our 20th wedding anniversary two days ago.

Elmer and the Schoolteacher lean over and rub noses. Everyone else is stunned.

Mayor – So after I have worried about you for 20 years. You show up here and let us know that you have been just fine and dandy?

Uncle Elmer – Well, basically yes. But we were forced against our will to come here. We should file some kind of lawsuit against those two.

Points to Shad and Samuel.

Fern – I think that would be just a mighty fine thing to do Elmer. Then every news reporter from here to kingdom come could go out to ya'lls nice and peaceful *spa* and interview you.

Schoolteacher – We really should get back to our guests. Nice seeing you all again.

Mayor – **Hold on just a minute!**

Those two stop dead in their tracks.

Mayor – You are not going anywhere. There is a missing persons report that is in need of some fixin' and I am just plain mad and don't want you to leave just yet. I feel that you owe us all an apology or something that tells us that you both are remorseful.

The schoolteacher and Elmer whisper to each other for a few seconds until the schoolteacher raises up her head and makes an announcement.

Schoolteacher – Since we have caused undo stress and harm to each of you, except Daley, we invite you all down to our Youkachokeka Spa and Resort for a day of mud packs, massages and imported coffees. What do you say? It retails for $400.00 a day per person.

Everyone talks at once and says yes, count me in, and point me in the direction of the swamp, I'm there.

Mayor – It seems that everyone here agrees with your offer. You will have to include Daley. If we all go and he doesn't he will make our lives more miserable than he already does.

Elmer nods and he shakes hands with his nephew, the Mayor. The couple leaves after a handshake or hug from each person. The rest all sit down and breathe a sigh of relieve. Then Samuel suddenly realizes something.

Samuel – Mayor are you going to make good on your promise? I solved the mystery of the swamp incident.

Lavana – We all want to know what you and the Mayor were whispering about before you took off three days ago. So tell us.

Mayor – It seems that Samuel has had his eye on something in my family for many years. He really wants…he wants…Cindy Lou to go on a real date with him.

Cindy Lou – You want to go out with me? I would love to go on a real date. No one has ever asked me before now.

Samuel – I'll go home and get cleaned up and I'll cook you dinner at my place.

Cindy Lou – I can hardly wait. See ya Samuel, I'll wait here for ya.

Samuel – Okay Cindy Lou, be back in a flash.

Samuel walks into the door then opens it. He's a bit on the nervous side. Everyone is shocked at the turn of events since three days ago.

Fern – I had better get home and get cleaned up. We've all been moping around for the last three days. Good luck on your date Cindy Lou.

Cindy Lou - Thanks Fern. Do you think that he might be the one for me?

Fern – I've learned over the years, that when you least expect something, that's when it will happen. This could be it Cindy Lou.

Fern leaves and Cindy Lou sits quietly and waits.

Daley – I think that I've had enough of this mushy love, dating, and marriage talk for one day. I'll be glad when today is over.

Shad – That reminds me. Mayor, you and I had an agreement and it's my turn to be Mayor for 24 hours.

Mayor – How could I forget that. I made that agreement when I thought that you wouldn't make it out alive. Okay, let's get it over with, starting…now. You have 24 hours. Behave or the deal is off!

Darren – Hotdog, I've waited my whole lifetime for an opportunity like this.

Shad – Why Darren, I'm the Mayor, not you.

Darren – Well you and I *are* best friends, so that makes me Mayor by association.

Shad – I'm too tired to argue with you Darren. I've got some things to take care of. Stay away from me. You are too gun-ho!

Darren – Oh man, I'll never make it in politics at this rate. Hey Shad where are you going? You're wasting valuable time.

Shad – Don't mess with me Darren. It has been a long three days. I do *not* need your help. I'll see you tomorrow.

Scene V

Narrator - The sleepy little town turns in for the night. Everything is quiet for the time being. Of course as the sun comes up, trouble creeps into the small town of Greenbow.

Fern shows up to go to work but no sign of Daley. She's looking around to see where he might be.

Fern – I need change for the register. Where could Daley be? He's never late.

The Mayor enters into the café.

Mayor – Hey Fern, where's that no good boss of yours?

Fern – I'm starting to get worried. He has never been late. He's too greedy. Always afraid that he might miss out on an order of toast or something.

Mayor – Have you checked out the back yet?

Fern – No, I'd better do that before I panic.

Before Fern leaves the cafe Lavana runs in all out of breath.

Mayor – Lavana what in the world is wrong?

Lavana – I saw, (*holding her stomach*) I saw Daley out back.

Fern – Is he all right?

Lavana – I think that he's dead Fern.

Mayor – Nobody go anywhere. Let me go look and then I'll find the Deputy. I may be gone a few minutes. Don't let anyone go out back.

Ya hear?

Fern and Lavana – We won't.

Fern – I hate to ask but what did Daley look like?

Lavana – He was laying on his side. His face was white like and he wasn't breathin' none.

Fern – How could this happen? I mean Daley doesn't have any friends but nobody hates his that bad. Do they?

Lavana – I couldn't say. I may never sleep again after what I saw.

Samuel and Cindy Lou walk into the café all lovey dovey. Samuel has lipstick kisses all over his face. They don't have a clue that someone's dead.

Fern – Hey guys, have y'all heard the news?

Samuel – We should be asking you the same question.

The two lovebirds rub noses.

Lavana – Between them and Daley, I think I'm gonna be sick.

Fern – Hush Lavana. You two don't know do you? There's been a death in Greenbow.

Cindy Lou – A *death*! Who in the world died?

Fern – Lavana found Daley in the alley dead as the road kill I use in my stew.

Cindy Lou – Oh my!

Samuel – How come I wasn't told?

Fern – The Mayor's been lookin' for ya. Where have you been anyway?

Samuel – Out.

Fern – You had better come up with a better story than that. As far as I'm concern we're all suspects.

Cindy Lou – I can not be a suspect. I wasn't in Greenbow until a few minutes ago.

Samuel – You hush now Cindy Lou. We'll explain our story later.

Lavana – I'd like to hear where you both have been. Maybe it'll take our minds off of Daley.

In walk the Mayor and Darren.

Mayor – There you are Samuel. I've looked all over for you. Where have you been? Never mind. You'll need to come out side with me and take a look at the body.

Darren – I'll go too Mayor. Since I'm partly the Mayor for about 10 more hours.

Mayor – Darren the Mayor situation is off for now. We may need a witness so come on. Dead bodies don't bother you do they?

Darren – I don't know yet.

The Mayor, Samuel and Darren disappear out the back way for a couple of minutes. While they're gone in walks Shad with the Schoolteacher and Elmer.

Fern – Hey there Shad. What are they doing back?

Shad – I saw them carrying a large package to their jeep and helped them load. What's everyone doing here so early?

Lavana – There's been a murder.
Fern – Now hold on Lavana. We don't know if Daley was murdered.

Shad – Daley's dead? Oh that's terrible! Does Samuel know?

Cindy Lou – Yes, he's out back right now lookin' at poor Daley.

Shad – Maybe I should go out there and see if they need any help.

About that time all three men come in talking at once. Arguing and biting each other's head off, so to speak.

Fern - Are y'all going to stop all that bickering and tell us what the problem is?

Mayor – He's gone.

Samuel – No Daley anywhere.

Lavana – I know what I saw. His eyes where open, but nobody was home!

Darren – Now calm down Lavana. Maybe you've been under a little stress lately.

Lavana – I have the most stress free life in this world. I know what I saw. Maybe you should ask these two that never come to town why their here.

Schoolteacher – We just thought that since you all knew where we lived we would pick up some supplies. That's all.

Elmer nods in agreement.

Mayor – We are going to have to have a statement from everybody here and see who was where. Maybe we can turn up something.

Samuel – I'll take everyone's statements Mayor.

Lavana – After Samuel and Cindy Lou left for their date last night I went home and went to bed. I was so worried about the guys the last three days I hadn't slept much. Once I knew they were home I slept like a baby. I live alone so you'll just have to believe me.

Samuel – Tell me exactly what you saw on your way to the café this morning.

Lavana – Since my house is a block away I always go the back way because it's faster. I fed my cat and locked my door. Then I headed over to the café to have a cup of coffee before I opened the shop for Cindy Lou. I just figured she would be late since she had a date and all. When I got to the back of the café there was Daley. He was laying on his side so I got a good look at his face. He was not a live.

Samuel – Okay Lavana. I may come back to you.

Samuel – Next is Fern.

Fern – My alibi is as bad as Lavana's. I went home and went right to bed for the same reason as Lavana. I got up early like I always do and came in to set up for breakfast and to put my stew on.

Samuel – Okay, next is Darren.

Darren – I hate to sound like a broken record but I went home early to make plans on being a Mayor for today. I figured that Shad would give in a little and I wanted to be prepared.

Samuel – Why do I believe you? Okay, Mayor what about you?

Mayor – My story is as lame as the others are.

Samuel – You went to bed early too?

Mayor – Yes I did.

Samuel – Cindy Lou, what about you?

Cindy Lou – I had a date with you. Please don't tell me that you forgot already?

Samuel – How could I forget the most exciting night of my life.

Mayor – Do you want to explain that Deputy? I'll have your job for that!

Samuel – Sir, Cindy Lou and I got engaged last night. We stayed up late and made wedding plans. I swear that's all we did. Right Cindy Lou?

Cindy Lou – Yes, that's all Daddy.

Mayor – Hot Dog, I may be Granddaddy someday yet!

Samuel – We've got to get back to business. Shad, you're next.

Shad – I was at home reading the by-laws of Greenbow. Sorry, just me and my dog.

Samuel – Okay last but not least, Elmer, speak up.

Elmer – Same as the others, I swear.

Fern – Beau has been out of town at a mechanics convention for the past few days. So he is the only one who has an alibi.

Samuel – How are we going to solve this case? We're going to need outside help. No body, lots of suspects and no weapon. If there was one?

Ending I

Narrator – We have a mess in Greenbow. Who would want Daley's body? No one even touched him when he was alive! Let's dissect these alibis. The bundle that the Schoolteacher and Elmer had was organic mud for the facials that they do at their spa. Besides they haven't been around Daley enough to develop a hatred for him. Let's check out Lavana. She really was asleep and never lies anyway. Fern did not like Daley. They fought on a daily basis. But remember, without Daley's café she is out of a job. She has to work. Shad was studying to be a Mayor. He wants to better himself and thought that this might be a good opportunity for him. Cindy Lou and Samuel actually ran off and got married last night. They are not planning on telling anyone. They are going to have a wedding for her Daddy and just have two wedding anniversaries each year. The Mayor was waiting up to see what time his daughter got home from her date. He fell asleep on his couch. He never knew what time they got home. Darren is a sleazy character. I know he was up to something. He never liked Daley. Daley used to bully him when they were growing up together. Darren was heading up to the café when he ran into Daley in the alley. They had words. Daley called Darren a coward and Darren lost his temper and hit Daley with his fist. He didn't realize how mad he was. Daley's head hit the water meter as he was falling to the grown. It broke his neck and he died instantly. Darren panicked and took the body down to the swamp. Darren is the guilty one!

Ending II

Narrator – Can you believe that someone would steal Daley's body? Yuck! Lavana is the only one who saw the body. Or is she? She really did go to sleep early the night before. What about Fern? She couldn't have done it. She needs her job and without Daley there is no café to work in. Let's move on to the Mayor. He waited up to see what time Samuel brought home Cindy Lou. After midnight he was so tired he fell asleep on the couch and never knew when the lovebirds got home. Then we have the lovebirds. They were down at the minister's home eloping and were going to keep it a secret and have a wedding soon anyway! Then there's Darren. He is a sleaze but he was snooping around the Mayor's office trying to break in to see what his duties really are. Darren's shoe size is higher than his IQ. What about those Swamp people? What are they doing back in town this soon? They have avoided Greenbow for twenty years. Well, come to find out Daley was one of their distributors. He filled all of there food orders. He had decided that since the Spa was doing so well he should get a larger percentage than he had agreed to many years before. Elmer and the Schoolteacher had had just about enough of Daley. So they snuck up on him behind the café and hit him on the head. He died before his head hit the ground. The bundle that Shad helped them load in their jeep was really Daley's body. Gross! The swamp people killed Daley!

Ending III

Narrator - You have heard everyone's alibis. It is amazing that they all seem guilty. Greenbow is a nice little town, except for Daley. The body did suddenly disappeared and that is odd. So did you think that maybe Daley is not dead at all? He is a mean and greedy person. Early that morning Daley decided that since the swamp incident was over he needed to do something to liven up the town. He made his face up real pale and put some fake blood across his forehead. Since Lavana always came to the café for coffee he knew exactly when she would come around the corner. What she saw was Daley pretending to be dead. As soon as everyone confessed their alibi's he shows up in the café and yells "Surprise!" Lavana fainted; Darren punched him in the nose. Now everything *is* back to normal. Fern has a job again. Shad is the Mayor for 8 more hours and Cindy Lou and Samuel are planning their wedding.

Play Suggestions for the Incident at the Road Kill Cafe

We had only one large hall to put the play on. We made the room the café and everyone "ran" into each other at the front or back entrances. We did have a large painted sign with "Road Kill Café" on it. It was painted on plywood.

Who ever plays Daley needs to enjoy playing a greedy annoying person. He tries to *cash* in on everyone's misfortune. When he has his t-shirts for sale, try and have a few made up that say "**20th Anniversary of the Youkachokea Swamp Incident**". It would be hilarious. Cindy Lou is always having a mindless conversation with herself. That character should have on too much make up and pearls and heels. She owns a beauty shop and over doing it would be an addition to her personality. Uncle Elmer has very little to say. This would be a good character for a grandpa type personality who wants to be in the play but does not like to memorize a lot. He should be in cover-alls or something country like. Darren is supposed to be handsome. Daley is a pain. I would part his hair down the middle and then slick it down. Maybe you could draw a thin mustache on him. We have a button maker at our church so we made up buttons that said *20th Anniversary of the Youkachokea Swamp Incident.* The characters gave the buttons out while they were doing their part. Cindy Lou made up business cards that she handed out the said *Cindy Lou's Beauty and Electrolysis Shop.*

When the swamp incident story is told, it could be printed on a menu because it would be a lot to memorize.

I have three different ending just in case you have more than one show. That way you can use a different ending each night.

During the play we had a group of five ladies that would stand up and sing between scenes. One song that was sung was called *Fern's Roadkill Stew*, sang to the tune of *Heart of My Heart,* the audience loved it. It went like this:

Fern's Road kill stew, we do so love that stew,
Fern's Road kill stew, comes back and repeats too!
It comes from the grill of your au-to-mobile,
It was tough and has bug eyes,
But oh how Fern can ten-der-ize!

Fern's Road kill stew, we do so love that stew,
To bad it had to die, to bad it had to die,
You know when heartburn comes,
With out a roll of tums,
You can't beat a bowl of Road kill stew,
*   Fern's Road kill stew...*

The character descriptions on the next page could be put in the program and left for the people to read while they wait for the play to start.

Fern Bailey – She was a bit wild as a teenager. Rumor has it she's a good shot from the back of a pick-up. Fern's always enjoyed cooking "native" dishes and has a great recipe for Armadillo Stew. She's got to watch her tips around Daley and her recipe, too!

Beau Stanley – Everyone likes Beau. (even Daley) Beau is sweet on Fern. But she said kissing <u>him</u> is like kissing her <u>brother</u>! He's getting tired of being single and told Lavana he's hopin' to meet someone special. Maybe at the mechanics convention.

Daley Bread – Daley is the manager of the Road Kill Café. He is mean and always looking for a new way to turn a buck. Back in his younger days he was quite a prankster. He even put sugar in Darren's gas tank. Most of Greenbow has a grudge against ol' Daley.

Samuel Bacon – Sam is the Deputy of Greenbow. The Sheriff quit and he is trying to keep the town in line. He has to constantly warn Daley about selling skunk meat in his café. You see there's a law still on the book that prohibits selling skunk inside the city limits. Daley's <u>always</u> causing him trouble. Samuel can't take much more!

Cindy Lou – Cindy Lou owns the local beauty shop next to the Road Kill Café. It's called the Hair and Polish Beauty Shop. She is also the town gossip. Guess you can tell why. Sam better watch out! That girl generates more energy talking than the Hoover Dam. Do you think she could stop talking long enough to kill someone?

Darren Finely – Darren can't seem to find his place in Greenbow. Maybe he should go into politics. Darren and Daley used to fight a lot when they were growing up. They were always trying to out do each other with the girls, in sports and as they got older, in business. Darren has always said that it was Fern, not Daley, that made the Road Kill Café successful. Do we detect jealousy?

Mayor Bradley – He is Cindy Lou's Daddy but can't stand to be in the same room with her for more than five minutes. He's got a decent *reputation, for a politician, that is. Just a word of warning. Don't <u>ever</u> get him mad. You know, like Daley did "disgracing his family name" by selling those T-shirts. When the Mayor gets mad, it ain't pretty.*

Lavana Webb – Lavana works with Cindy Lou at the Beauty Shop. She's "new" in town. Only been in Greenbow 19 years. Sometimes Lavana's kindness will drive you to the brink of wanting to grab her by the throat and squeeze real hard. You get the idea, don't you?

Shad Watson – Shad has been hiding out around the swamp most of his life. He can't seem to stay out of trouble. Actually, he's one of the smartest people in Greenbow. Rumor has it his IQ is over 100! That really bothers Daley.

Elmer & the Schoolteacher – They were "missing" for so long. Did you notice how quickly they made themselves right at home in Greenbow? Darren saw them paying-off Daley. Could they be in business together? Who could trust Daley? Was Daley trying to turn another buck?

Narrator – He couldn't have done it. He has a nighttime job as a DJ at the local radio station.

Suzann Carr

RAWHIDE

Written by:
Suzann Carr

Suzann Carr

Rawhide©

Liza Nellie-Seems to be sweet as pie and cute as a Button. Like I said, seems to be!

Duke Sargent-He is just lookin' for a wife to settle down with and have a passel of young 'uns. Will he ever find true love?

Sheriff Nunnley- He just can't put two and two together. The Sheriff has a sixth grade education. Not your smartest man in Rawhide. But he is your most honest. Honest!

Bill "Willie" Clanton-This man is always up to no good. Slick Willie just got back into town after living in Washington D.C. for the past eight years. He's very sneaky and tries to put the blame on the Republicans, I mean someone else.

Sarah Jane- Married at 17 and by the time she was 30 she had 10 children. Now a widow, she runs the towns dry good store. Her children are grown and moved off and she has ill feelings towards Willie. (Who doesn't)

Sally Jewel- Miss Jewel is the owner of the local Saloon. She is mighty friendly and loves her work. She has managed to become the wealthiest person in Rawhide.

Deputy Clyde-He hasn't quite learned to maneuver his long legs. Always tripping over something or someone. The Sheriff's Brother-In-Law.

The Mayor-Tries to keep the town running smooth. Especially when they have the annual ho-down. Usually things don't ever run smooth in Rawhide.

Sissy: Waitress at the local café. She is a hard working gal with younger siblings to support.

Narrator: He narrates, what else?

Welcome to Rawhide! This little town has some problems. There are men that need wives. The Sheriff tries hard and the Deputy is just hard to describe! (Don't get too close to Clyde, he can't keep a hold on his gun.) We have a scoundrel all the way from Washington D.C. and an annual Ho-Down that the women leave much to be desired. Watch out for Sarah Jane's buckshot and Slick Willie's pick up lines(Clydes are worse) and chances are there just might be a murder.

This play read out loud without any breaks is 27 minutes long.

Scene I

Liza and Duke are walking down Main Street.

Liza: Well Duke, it's that time of year again. I can't believe it's been a whole year since the last Ho-Down.

Duke: I know it Liza. I still haven't found me a woman to marry. I'm getting up there in years. I want to settle down. Gosh Liza, I want a home filled with children.

Liza: What do you mean you're getting up there in years! Now you're only twenty years old and so am I. We grew up together! I am ***still very young!***

Duke: I'm surprised you aren't settled down and married. All your friends are married and have at least two kids of their own. What are ya waiting for?

Liza: I just know that some day the perfect gentleman will come through this here town and sweep me off my feet! I don't want to settle down with just any ole man. I want to marry for LOVE.

Duke: I wouldn't hold my breath if I were you Liza. This here is a *very* small town. Your choices are limited and you know it.

Liza: Well, and so are yours. At this rate you and I will never get married. I'd better go. I need to get ready for the dance tonight. You know, just in case Mr. Perfect comes to town.

Duke: Sure thing Liza. Save a dance for me.

Liza: You bet I will. See ya Duke.

Sheriff Nunnelly sees Duke and walks over to speak to him.

Sheriff: Hey there Duke. You ready for tonight? I hear they got women coming over from Hidden Valley. Single women!

Duke: I'm about as ready as I'll ever be, I guess. Hidden Valley huh. Are they pretty?

Sheriff: Who cares as long as they're breathing!

Duke: You got that right. At my age, I'm not that picky.

Sheriff: I need to talk to you. It's about Bill Clanton.

Duke: Why are ya bringing Ole Willie up after all these years? He's been gone for over eight years now.

Sheriff: I got word from a source that he is due back this way any day now. You know he told Liza a long time ago that when she was grown he would be back to claim her as his own. I think that could just happen. You know she inherited all that land when her Daddy died last year. I bet Clanton heard about that.

Duke: Well, heck fire that's all I need. I've got to worry about her when all these pretty women, I mean single women from Hidden Valley are coming to the dance. Okay, I'll look out for Liza. You can count on me. I guess I can live with being single another year.

Sheriff: Thanks. I need all the help I can get. Oh no, here comes Clyde.

Deputy Clyde: Hey Sheriff, I hear you was lookin for me.

Clyde: *Clyde trips and drops his gun on the ground. (picks it up, looks at the pistol, peering into the barrel and says)* It's okay!

Sheriff: How many times have I told you, don't look at the barrel of your gun! I oughta take that thing away from you before you shoot someone!

And where in tarnation have you been? And don't tell me at Sally Jewel's Saloon.

Clyde: *Clyde thinks a minute, looks puzzled and says*, "which one of those questions you want me to answer first, sheriff?"

Sheriff: Why do I bother with you? If you weren't my wife's brother's cousin, I would have ran you off a long time ago. Now here's what I have in store for you. I need you to pay attention tonight at the dance.

Clyde: That won't be a problem Sheriff. I hear we got girls coming to town that might be just a bit hard up for a husband and I plan to save one of 'em from the single life they've been leadin.

Sheriff: (*Sarcastically*) yea, I'm sure they'll be fightin' over who gets to marry you first. Sorry to burst your bubble Clyde but you have to be on the look out for Bill Clanton. No wife hunting for you tonight.

Clyde: Willie! You mean that wild, crazy, womanizer is comin back to Rawhide on the only night I **might** find me a wife! I could just kill that slick Willie. He broke Bessy's heart when he left her at the altar. He left on bad terms and should never come this way again.

Sheriff: Watch your mouth Clyde. Somebody might hear you and think you mean it. If anyone has a right to getting rid of Willie it would be Sarah Jane. He promised her oldest daughter his hand in marriage and he left her at the altar. Sarah Jane is likely to but some buckshot where it counts.

Clyde: I had better make sure she has some in stock. If not, I do. I'll see ya at the ho-down. (*Spins around, bumps into sheriff on way out, says* "I'm okay, you okay?"

Sheriff: (*Slaps at him*) Now go on and get outta here, and watch your mouth, now ya hear!

Clyde: *Clydeenters Sarah Jane's store. Knocks over a stack of can goods. Drops his hat. (picks it up and says)* It's okay!

Sarah Jane: Well hello there Sonny, now that you've rearranged my store, what can I do for ya?

Clyde: Hello there Miss Sarah Jane. You look finer than frog hair.

Sarah Jane: Now don't you come in here and use that fancy talk with me. What can I get for ya?

Clyde: I ain't buying today Ma'am. I've got some bad news to tell ya.

Sarah Jane: It ain't one of my kin is it? They all moved on but I still get telegrams on occasions. Did one of them send one?

Clyde: No ma'am, but the Sheriff just told me that Willie Clanton is headin back into town soon. I thought you might want to know.

Sarah Jane: Oh he is, is he? I've waited a long time to see his face again. I had better check my shotgun and make sure my buckshot is in it. It won't kill 'em, just make him wish he was dead.

Clyde: I told the Sheriff that's what you would do. You sure are predictable Miss Sarah Jane.

Sarah Jane: Is that so? I might just surprise you this time.

Clyde: Don't do anything to break the law now. The Sheriff is trying to clean up Rawhide.

Sarah Jane: What's takin him so long? My Husband Joe (*takes off bonnet and places over her chest & Clyde does the same with his hat*) God rest his soul, was as slow as a mule on a Monday morning. He managed to father ten children and get this here store going. (*pauses*) I think that we need a new Sheriff.

Clyde: You're just upset Miss Sarah Jane. If we get a new Sheriff I lose my job. Besides, nobody else wants the job. *(heading out the door)* I've got to run. Will I see you tonight?

Sarah Jane: If the Lord's a willin and the creeks don't rise you will. *(Muttering under her breath)* I think *I* would make a perfect Sheriff. This town can't be harder to control than those ten kids of mine!

Scene II

Sissy is waiting tables at the Rawhide café and in walks Willie.

Willie: Hello there pretty lady.

Sissy: Hello there yourself, I'm busy here what can I get for you?

Willie: First of all I need your name.

Sissy: The population in this town is about 75. Ask anyone they'll tell ya. You ordering or just here to try my patience?

Willie: Rawhide sure has changed. What happened to all the *friendly* people? Are any left?

Sissy: It's the annual ho-down and we're short handed and I'm tired. Wave me down if you need to order. *(Sissy walks off to wait on a real customer)*

In walks Sally Jewel, dressed to kill and to flaunt her wealth.

Willie: Sally Jewel? Is that really you? You sure have changed. You were poor as a church mouse last time I saw you. What's with all that flashy jewelry?

Sally Jewel: It sure has been a long time there Slick Willie. Since you've been gone I've become the richest woman in town. I own the Saloon. Miners come from all over to my place. Not minors like children, you know, miners like, men who spend time in the dark, digging and working with their hands and getting all sweaty and… *(getting faint and fanning herself)* Well you know!

Willie: Not bad, are you seeing anyone Sally? Maybe we could get together later?

Sally Jewel: Can't do that Willie. My place is busy in the evenings and I've got to keep an eye on things.

Willie: That's too bad. I could use a gal who's loaded like, I mean lovely as you on my arm. Nice seeing ya again, call me if you get lonely.

Sally Jewel: Maybe, like when Sarah Jane quits holding a grudge against you, and that day will never come!

Willie: Sarah Jane is still living? I thought she kicked the bucket. That's why I came back. I was going to try and sell my Granddaddy's old place. Now I have to deal with that old coot too!

Sally Jewel: Good luck selling that old sorry piece of land and watch your backside. She's got plenty of buckshot on her shelves. *(Laughs at Bill as he leaves the café)*

Sissy: Can I get you anything Sally?

Sally Jewel: I could use a cup of coffee. Thanks. You know Sissy, you're one of the few women in this town that is nice to me.

Sissy: I work hard to take care of my brother and sister. I know what it's like to be hungry. I won't do what you do for a living, but I know you work hard too.

Sally Jewel: It's mighty nice of you to say that.

Sissy: Well, don't get all mushy on me. You know I work on tips. Don't forget to over tip your waitress.

Sally Jewel: Now that's the Sissy we all know and love around here!

In walks Duke and Sally Jewel takes notice.

Sally Jewel: Hey there Duke. *(she pats the chair next to her)* Why don't you come and sit over here?

Duke: Sure Sally. You doin all right?

Sally Jewel: I am now. Tell me Duke, how come you haven't settled down yet?

Duke: I'm still looking for just the right woman to grow old with. I haven't found her yet Sally.

Sally Jewel: What do you mean you haven't found her. She's been right in front of you for all these years! I can't believe you haven't noticed.

Duke: *(deep in thought)* You know something Sally, you just might have a point there. I've got to go. *(Kisses her on the cheek and runs out of the restaurant)*

Sally Jewel: Well how do you like that? Maybe he is sweet on me after all? I sure wouldn't mind growing old with Duke.

Scene III

Narrator: The dance is about to begin. The Mayor is introducing the homely, I mean lovely young maidens from Hidden Valley. All are present to see if Willie really is back in town.

Mayor: I want to welcome everyone to our 10th annual Ho-Down. It is great to have our neighboring towns come and spend their money, I mean time here in Rawhide. Be sure and check out the bake sale over at the church on your way home tonight. All the proceeds are going to build an Out House for Grandpa Jenkins. And we all know that since his last one blew up he is in need of a new as soon as possible! I told the darn fool not to light a match in there! Well, anyway thank y'all for coming!

In walks Willie and the whole town moans. Here comes the Sheriff with Clyde at his heals. Clyde trips and bumps into the Sheriff.

Clyde: I'm okay, you okay sheriff?

The Sheriff takes off his hat and hits Clyde with it.

Sheriff: Tell me Clyde, have you had any troubles this evening? Did Sarah Jane say anything? Does Liza know Willie is here? Are those women from Hidden Valley or Siberia?

Clyde: Hold on a minute Sheriff! No trouble, yes Sarah Jane had plenty of buckshot and Liza doesn't have a clue, as usual. Your guess is as good as mine about those women. They do look like they could handle living in the country. Anything else cause I want to go dance. Those gals look older than I expected. Oh well, at least they're here.

Sheriff: Go ahead and have a good time, thanks for helping me out here.

Clyde: Yea, yea whatever, *(talking to a "sort of" young thing across the room)* hey there would you like to arm wrestle?

Clyde greets one of the "single" women.

Clyde: Why hello there young lady. I bet your legs are tired, cause you've been running through my mind all day.

The young lady blushes and off they go to dance.

Liza walks in and sees Willie. She can't believe her eyes. Is it really him? About that time Sarah Jane sees Liza see Willie.

Liza: Why Bill Clanton, it's been years since I've laid eyes on you. You look wonderful! Where's the Mrs.? Or did you ever marry?

Willie: I told you that I would be back for you Liza. I knew that you would grow up to be beautiful woman. Sure enough, you're the prettiest thing I've seen in a long time. You didn't go and get married did you?

Sarah Jane can't help but over hear and voice her opinion.

Sarah Jane: It's been a long time Willie. What lies are ya tellin that poor gal. Maybe that you might marry her! Take it from me missy. This man ain't any good. He left my Bessy at the altar and left town the next day. He has the nerve to show up after eight years of hiding out back east. I hear ya missed the draft for the civil war. What'd ya do to get out of that? Stump your toe?

Willie: Look Sarah Jane, I'm sorry about your daughter and all, I had something suddenly come up and couldn't make the wedding.

Liza: Come to think of it, he never asked me to marry him Miss Sarah Jane, just that he would come back for me.

Clyde has since switched dancing partners.

Clyde: Kiss me if I'm wrong, but haven't we met before?

Dance partner blushes and giggle and the two keep on dancing.

Duke shows up to ask Liza to dance.

Duke: Liza do you want to dance with me? This may be the last song.

Liza: Sure Duke. This night has been such a let down. I'm sadder than a hound dog after huntin season. There's never nothing to do in this hick town. Come on Duke let's dance.

Clyde is trying out his third dance partner.

Clyde: Darlin If I could rewrite the alphabet, I'd put U and I together.

Dance Partner: Oh Clyde, you say the nicest things.

Clyde: Beauty is in the eye of the beholder and I hope to be holdin you tonight!

Clyde and the young lady with the "beauty" mark by her nose dance the last dance at the 10th annual Ho-Down.

Scene IV

Sarah Jane: I had better get over and man that bake sale before Clyde trips over the table.

Clyde: Did you say something Miss Sarah Jane?

Sarah Jane: uh yea Clyde, why don't you go and help clean up the dance area? And stay away from the bake sale, ya hear?

Clyde: All right, you don't have to yell. Hey where did all those gals from Hidden Valley run off to?

Sarah Jane: They went to get ready for bed. I'm sure they're all worn out from listening to your sweet talk. If you have to know where they're all staying. It's at the local motel.

Clyde: I hope to see 'em in the morning before they leave town.

Sarah Jane: I'm sure you still have a shot at one of 'em Clyde. You were one of the few who showed any interest. You could probably take your pick.

Clyde: I wish that was true. The cute one, you know with the beauty mark on the side of her nose. I think she's a good cook. She's the cook at the No-tell restaurant in Hidden Valley.

Sarah Jane: *(Talking to the audience)* If that's a beauty mark you can just call me Mae West. Oh well, he wouldn't believe me anyways.

Clyde: I wish I had a library card Miss Sarah Jane.

Sarah Jane: What in the world fer?

Clyde: Cause I'd like to check Miss Beauty Mark out, for the rest of my life.

Miss Sarah Jane: Go get some sleep boy! See ya tomorrow Clyde.

Clyde: *(dreamy eyed like and sighs)* Sure thing Miss Sarah Jane, see ya.

Clyde leaves and Willie comes to the bake sale.

Willie(Bill): How's it going Miss Sarah Jane?

Sarah Jane: If you're talking about the bake sale fine, if you're talking about you coming back in town, not too good.

Bill: Can't we call a truce? It's been a long time Miss Sarah Jane. I was a lot younger and had a lot less smarts.

Sarah Jane: I don't know Willie. It's tough raisin' younguns and then when *someone* breaks their heart, well the parents suffer right along with the child.

Bill: I never had kids so I guess I don't fully understand.

Sarah Jane: I tell you what. If you buy what's left of this bake sale so we can get Grandpa Jenkins back in business again with a new out house I might start a little forgiving.

Bill: Ya mean it Miss Sarah Jane? Sure I would be glad to help out. How come everyone is in such a hurry to get Grandpa Jenkins out house built.

Sarah Jane: Oh, that's simple. He keeps comin over to my house everyday and night to use mine. I headed up this bake sale so he could stay home and use his own.

Bill: I can't say that I blame you. Maybe we could build Grandpa Jenkins a double wide outhouse!

Sarah Jane: After you pay me for all of these goodies, we just might be able too.

Scene V(1st ending)

Duke and Liza enter the Rawhide Café.

Duke: Guess what everybody? Liza and I got married last night! I'm not going to grow old alone. Am I honey?

Liza: No you're not. I should have married you a long time ago. You've been my best friend since we were kids.

Sarah Jane hugs the happy couple.

Sarah Jane: I have an announcement too. I've decided to give up my revenge on Willie. I just know that someday he'll get what's coming to him. I know longer care about making him pay. I can't live my life plotting against that sorry excuse for a man.

Sally Jewel: That's a good thing, you would just be wastin your time. He is already getting what's coming to him. He is so broke he couldn't afford to pay attention! I had to buy him a meal and a drink at my place last night.

Sheriff and Clyde enter the café.

Sheriff: I have some bad news for some and good news for others. Early this morning Sissy was found murdered. She had been hit over the head and all the money from the café was stolen. I need to find out where you all were last night after the dance.

First ending

Narrator: We all know that Slick Willie was broke and is the first person that comes to mind when there is a murder. Sissy did not care for Willie either. Willie was at Sally Jewel's Saloon and has a room full of witnesses to prove his where abouts. Liza and Duke had already run off to get married and they also have an alibi from the preacher in Hidden Valley that married them. Clyde had a date with a nice young uh thing, who may be interested in marriage. Of course it depends on his future with the law enforcement in Rawhide. Now where was Sarah Jane? How could we blame a murder on such a decent human. Besides, she had to run the bake sale at the church after the dance was over. That leaves the Mayor and Sally Jewel. The Mayor was seen at Sally Jewel's singing on a Karaoke machine after drinking a few too many Shirley Temples. But what about Sally Jewel? It seems that she did not have as much money as everyone thought. After some investigation, it was said that she had a bad habit of trusting Willie. He had invested all of her money in an Ostrich ranch in Robstown, Texas. She killed Sissy to get the money so she could keep her saloon open and her reputation in tact!

Scene V (2nd ending)

Duke and Liza enter the Rawhide Café.

Duke: Guess what everybody? Liza and I got married last night! I'm not going to grow old alone. Am I honey?

Liza: No you're not. I should have married you a long time ago. You've been my best friend since we were kids.

Sarah Jane hugs the happy couple.

Sarah Jane: I have an announcement too. I've decided to give up my revenge on Willie. I just know that someday he'll get what's coming to him. I know longer care about making him pay.

Sally Jewel: That's a good thing because he is so broke he couldn't afford to pay attention! I had to buy him a drink at my place last night.

Sheriff and Clyde enter the café.

Sheriff: I have some bad news for some and good news for others. Early this morning Willie was found murdered. He had been hit over the head and left in the area where the dance was held. I need to find out where you all were last night after the dance.

Second ending

Narrator: Liza and Duke had already run off to get married and they also have an alibi from the preacher in Hidden Valley that married them. Clyde had a date with a nice young lady who may be interested in marriage. It depends on his future with the law enforcement in Rawhide. Now where was Sarah Jane? How could we blame a murder on such a decent human. Besides she had to run the bake sale at the church after the dance was over. That leaves the Mayor, Sissy and Sally Jewel. The Mayor was seen at Sally Jewel's singing on a Karaoke machine after drinking a few too many Shirley Temples. But what about Sally Jewel? It seems that she did not have as much money as everyone thought. After some investigation, it was said that she had a bad habit of trusting Willie. He had invested all of her money in an Ostrich ranch in Robstown, Texas. She couldn't kill Willie because they know that it would take both of them to sell off that bird ranch. Sissy had been pretty upset when Willie was flirting with her at the Café. She was cleaning up after closing and in walks Willie. He would not leave and wanted to know what time Sally Jewel took her money to the bank the next day. When he turned his back she hit him with an iron skillet and accidentally killed him. Sissy panicked and left the body by the dance area so it would look like it happened somewhere besides the café.

Scene V(3rd ending)

Duke and Liza come in the restaurant with their arms around each other.

Duke: Hey everybody, guess what? Liza and I were married last night*!* *(Everyone cheers)*

Liza: I was just about to give up on men altogether. Not that there were any men in Rawhide to give up on.

Sally Jewel: I can't believe this. *(Under her breath)* I thought that he was sweet on me!

Duke: I realized that after you told me to look right in front me I did and there was Liza. *(Looks at Liza all dreamy eyed)*

Sarah Jane: Don't that beat all. I want to purpose a toast to the newlyweds.

Everyone raises their glasses and say's to the newlyweds, "To the newlyweds". Enters the Mayor.

Mayor: We've got a problem. There's been a murder. Willie was found murdered. *(The Sheriff & Clyde are shocked)* The Sheriff and Clyde need to talk to each and everyone of you.

Third Ending

Narrator: Now it all seems that everyone hated Slick Willie. We know that Duke and Liza were in Hidden Valley getting married. They have the license to prove it and the Minister will back up their stories. Then there is Sissy. She sure didn't like him coming on to her at the restaurant. But she was seen at home with her siblings fixing them dinner. Who is left but Sarah Jane? Sarah Jane was heading up the bake sale trying to keep the pies from being stolen by all the younguns running around. There is someone we forgot, Sally Jewel. Come to find out, before Slick Willie left town, he and Sally Jewel had made a business deal. He married her so that she could get a loan to start up her saloon business. Now Bill was back to collect his share of the profits. She thought it was time to get rid of ole Willie. She did get rid of him by putting poison in his meal he had at the saloon last night. The bottle of poison was found in her office in the bottom of her cash box in her desk.

Rawhide Suggestions

Liza is a very pretty lady and has had an easy life. She could have a parasol to match her dress.

Duke is tall and handsome. The friendly type.

Clyde could steal the show if you let him. When he drops his gun have someone pop a balloon back stage. Set up a pyramid of boxes for him to knock over when he is in Miss Sarah Jane's store. Every time he trips he could rub his hands over his chest and every time say, "nothings broken".

Willie could be wearing a bow tie that is made out of a patriotic material. He did just get back from D.C.!

You will need some extra girls for the dance. It would be funny if you had some grandmotherly types to volunteer to be the single women from Hidden Valley. Or you could have about four men who would not make pretty women dress up as women for the dance. It would send the audience rolling in the aisles. Be sure and put a fake mole on the side of one of their noses. These Hidden Valley ladies do not even have to speak. Only the one with the "beauty" mark has one line.

If you are serving dinner, it could be served between scenes III and IV. Or if you have a musical act to perform that would also be a good time for an intermission.

The character descriptions on the next page could be put in the program and left for the people to read while they wait for the play to start.

Liza Nellie

I could not have possibly have killed anyone. Why I am too nice a person. Besides I have my marriage license and the minister to prove that I was not even in town when the murder happened. Duke and I were just a little too busy to be out trying to end someone's life. Go pick on someone else! Sally Jewel wears her dresses a little too low for me. Maybe she did it!

Duke Sargent

I have been too busy looking for a wife. I do not have that kind of personality to take someone's life. You can ask the minister that married me and my new lovely wife, Liza or you can call her the Mrs.! Besides everyone knows that I was in Hidden Valley. Liza and I have the marriage license to prove it! So there!

Sheriff Nunnley

How can you accuse the law of doing such a horrible deed? I was with Clyde trying to clean up the mess everyone left after the dance. Those Hidden Valley girls are not the neatest people I've seen. Anyway, I have to up hold the law, not break it.

Bill "Slick Willie" Clanton

Has anyone ever mentioned how I got the name Slick Willie? You probably thought the worst when you first heard it. See when I was a little boy I won the "catch a grease pig" contest. My nick name was Willie at the time and it changed to "Slick Willie" after that. So I'm not as bad as you may have thought. How could a kid who won a pig contest do anything wrong. You need to go pick on a republican, I mean someone else.

Sarah Jane
Now how could a woman who has given birth to ten children go and take someone's life. You know that I would like to hurt *Willie. If I wanted to kill Willie or who ever, I would have had more than buck shot in my shot gun. I hit what I aim for and I would rather hurt than kill.*

Sally Jewel
I am just too busy with my "business" to go out and try and kill someone. I do not even have the time to try and plot a way to kill someone. I am the wealthiest woman in Rawhide and have a reputation to keep. There is nothing else I need in the world. I have everything I want.

Deputy Clyde
I don't know why anyone would suspect me. I can hardly write my own name. I had to get Miss Sarah Jane to type this alibi up for me. I am just a sweet, kind Deputy who's mission in life is to find me a wife who can cook. Killing someone isn't even on my list of things to do. I think you had better consider someone else.

Sissy
I don't have time to kill someone. I am at the restaurant all day. I have a brother and sister who depend on me. How can I find the time to kill someone when I barely have time to do the laundry and fix dinner when I get home from waiting on tables. I think you need to look into someone else's life, not mine.

Suzann Carr

The Castlemeyer Fortune

Written By: Suzann Carr

▶ The Castlemeyer Fortune

Mrs. Emily Castlemeyer-She is a very wealthy widow with no living relatives. *(That she knows of!)* Not one of your nicest people. She is very ill and must leave all of that money to somebody. In her opinion, the worst thing about dying is that she can't take it with her!

Melvin Drysdale-He has been the Castlemeyer banker for years. A trustworthy friend and businessman. Or is he? He sleeps on a mattress stuffed with $5 bills.

Monte Cello-He met Mrs. Castlemeyer at a dinner party last year. He keeps coming around like a lost dog. She can't seem to be rid of him. At least he's handsome.

Yvette-Every rich lady needs a french maid. This one is a character. She has a very thick accent. She's missing a few marbles. No one is sure how she keeps her job.

William Trust-The family attorney. Always checking on Mrs. Castlemeyers well being. What a good friend. Right, did you not read his title, Attorney!

Nurse Hatchet-The nurse that William Trust hired to see that all of Mrs. Castlemeyers needs are taking care of.

Dr. Feelgood-I'm not sure that I would "feelgood" if this man was my Doctor. Maybe someone needs to checkout his credentials.

Muffin Castlemeyer-Relative of Mrs. Castlemeyer? You'll find out soon. Read on!

Narrator: Still narrating.

The Castlemeyer Fortune

We have a widow without any heirs. We also have a whole bunch of greedy people just doing all that they can to try and keep Mrs. Castlemeyer happy, which is next to impossible. Who can really be trusted? Why does Monte keep coming around? With 500 million dollars at stake you can bet your bottom dollar that there will be a murder. Everyone is a suspect in this thriller.

Read out loud with no breaks this play is 21 minutes long.

Scene I

Mrs. Castlemeyer is bed ridden and can't seem to get Yvette's attention.

Mrs. Castlemeyer: Yvette, get in here! *(muttering)* Where in the world has that girl been? I pay her good money. Never around when I need her.

Yvette: Oui Madame, did you call? *(curtsies)*

Mrs. Castlemeyer: Did I call? Did I call? HELLO! I have been calling for over five minutes! I am sure that the entire household knows that I've been calling for you. Where have you been?

Yvette: I was making your tea *just* the way you like it Madame.

Mrs. Castlemeyer: Yvette, I don't even like tea, I drink coffee. After all of this time you can't remember that?

Yvette: I was so nervous when I heard you calling that I dropped the tea kettle and spilled it all on the kitchen floor. It is such a mess. Please forgive me Madame!

Mrs. Castlemeyer: Now that you messed up the tea, why don't you go and make a pot of coffee! I called because my attorney, Mr. William Trust is due over here soon and I need you to straighten my bed for me. I do not want him to think that I am not well taken care of.

Yvette: Oui Madame, I will help you. *(Curtsies)*

(Knock on the door)

Mrs. Castlemeyer: Oh goodness, he must be early. Don't just stand their, go answer the door!

Yvette: Good morning Mr. Trust. Mrs. Castlemeyer is expecting you.

William Trust: Thank you Yvette. *(Looking at Yvette closely)* You are a very pretty lady. How would you like to have dinner at my place later on?

Yvette: Why, do you need me to cook for you? I make a very good pot of tea.

William Trust: Uh no Yvette. I thought that we could go, you know, on a date.

Yvette: I do not understand. But if you need someone to cook and clean I will help you.

William Trust: Never mind Yvette. Please let Mrs. Castlemeyer know that I am here.

William shakes his head and Yvette gives Mr. Trust a strange look. Yvette shows him to the bedroom. She leaves him alone with Mrs. Castlemeyer.

William Trust: If I didn't know any better, Emily, I would think that you have taken a turn for the better since I saw you last. *(holds her hand and kisses it)*

Mrs. Castlemeyer: If I didn't know better I would think that you were kissing up to a very rich, sick old lady! I need to know, did you draw up the papers that I asked you about?

William Trust: I did, Emily. I still think that you are making a rash decision. Are you sure you want your last Will and Testament to read this way? It is far from proper.

Mrs. Castlemeyer: When you have as much money as I do, proper does not figure in. I don't think that I have a choice in the matter. Will you be able to make it to dinner tomorrow evening?

William Trust: I would not miss it for all the diamonds in South Africa. You can take that as an RSVP.

Mrs. Castlemeyer: I appreciate that William. I need to know that I can count on you in my time of need. Everyone has already replied to my invitations. I heard from them all very quickly. Do you think that they know about my illness?

William Trust: The way that Monte has been moping around town they have to know that something is amiss. I am sure they are all curious about what's going on in your life. You are by far the wealthiest person in Park Hills.

Mrs. Castlemeyer: You are right. I should have realized that I would be missed by all of my dear friends. Of course if I didn't have all of this money, they would not walk across a street to speak to me. Money does have its advantages, William.

William Trust: Yes it does. I had better get back to my office. I will see you tomorrow evening and I won't forget the revised will.

Mrs. Castlemeyer: Please don't! The whole evening will be for nothing if that minor detail is left out. Ta Ta, Will.

William Trust: Ta Ta to you too! *(rolls his eyes and leaves)*

Enters Monte Cello.

Monte: Why Emily, who was that I saw driving away just now?

Mrs. Castlemeyer: None of you business, that's who. Who let you in anyway? I instructed my staff that you were not to be permitted on my Estate. How did you get in here?!

Monte: You know that you don't mean that, Emily. Now lean over here and give me a little kiss. *(Leans over Emily)*

Mrs. Castlemeyer: *(Trying to back away)* I'm not going to kiss you. Are you crazy? Did you not hear me? I know I'm old but I'm far from stupid. I wanted to know who let you in?

Monte: Now Now, Emily. *(patting her hand and then kisses it)* don't go and get yourself all upset now. I will let myself out and I can't wait to see *you* tomorrow evening at the dinner party.

Monte leaves and Mrs. Castlemeyer yells across her room

Mrs. Castlemeyer: **You are not invited you nut case.** *(muttering)* I can't believe that he has the nerve to treat me this way. You can bet he is not going to get away with it this time.

Enters Nurse Hatchet carrying a tray. Checks Mrs. Castlemeyer's pulse.

Nurse Hatchet: Good morning, Mrs. Castlemeyer. I trust that you slept well.

Mrs. Castlemeyer: Why yes I did. I'm not sure why but I did rest well.

Nurse Hatchet: I put a little something in your tea last night to relax you. You seem so tense I thought it would do you good.

Mrs. Castlemeyer: That's funny, I didn't drink any tea last night.

Enters Yvette to check on Mrs. Castlemeyer.

Yvette: Madame, can I get you anything?

Mrs. Castlemeyer: Yvette, did you have some tea last night before bedtime?

Yvette: Oui, and I slept like a baby. You should try tea Madame. It will do wonders for you.

Yvette exits.

Nurse Hatchet: I guess I had better watch what cup I spike.

Mrs. Castlemeyer: I think I will have Yvette taste all of my food and drink from now on! I do have some paper work to do. Will you excuse me please?

Nurse Hatchet: Why of course, Mrs. Castlemeyer. I will be near by if you need me.

Mrs. Castlemeyer: *(Muttering)* I'm sure you will.
Talking to herself: I do not know what I'm going to do. I can not seem to find a living relative that I can leave all of my money to. If I had my choice I would just take it with me!

Nurse Hatchet and Dr. Feelgood were listening in on Mrs. Castlemeyer's conversation.

Nurse Hatchet: Did you hear that, Doctor?

Dr. Feelgood: I sure did. I can't believe she has no one left!

Nurse Hatchet: Well maybe she does have someone. If you know what I mean.

Dr. Feelgood: Let's see what we can do.

The Doctor and Nurse leave the scene and enters Yvette.

Yvette: Madame, can I get you anything?

Mrs. Castlemeyer: What have you been cooking in the kitchen?

Yvette: I have made Steak Tar Tar and Escargot.

Mrs. Castlemeyer: So you mean to tell me that I am having *Raw meat and snails* dinner!

Yvette: Oui, it is wonderful. Would you like me to bring up a tray? I made a pot of tea.

Mrs. Castlemeyer: No thanks. Get me the phone book. I give up on you. I'm ordering a pizza.

Yvette: That sounds wonderful. Can you get anchovies on my half?

Mrs. Castlemeyer: You have no half. No eat your raw meat and snails.

Yvette exits and Mrs. Castlemeyer starts talking to herself again.

Mrs. Castlemeyer: I hope that child learns something before I go. She is going to have to make her way in the world somehow. I sure do worry about her.

There is a knock on the door.

Yvette: Mrs. Castlemeyer, Mr. Drysdale is here to see you.

Mrs. Castlemeyer: Please show him in.

Yvette: Oui Madame.

Mr. Drysdale: Hello Emily. You look lovely this afternoon. How are you feeling?

Mrs. Castlemeyer: Well, I'm not dead yet, Melvin. I know why you're here. When I die you're worried about all of my money leaving your precious bank.

Mr. Drysdale: Now Emily, you know how much I care for you.

Mrs. Castlemeyer: Yes I do. And it is about 500 million dollars worth of caring. So I guess you care a *great deal*!

Mr. Drysdale: There's no reason to be in a snit. I do have respect for large sums of money. I'm only human you know. I just wanted to check on your vitals, I mean to check on your health. I feel better knowing that you are still feisty and ready to do battle. See you tomorrow night, Emily.

Mrs. Castlemeyer: Sure thing, Melvin, see you tomorrow. *Talking to the audience.* That man makes me look good. He is one greedy guy!

Mrs. Castlemeyer waves him off and goes back to her paperwork.

Scene II

Narrator: Everyone sure is excited about this dinner party. (Everyone except Monte) Let's sit back and watch how everyone reacts to the Mrs. when she make her announcement.

The guests are starting to show and Yvette pushes Mrs. Castlemeyer in her wheelchair to the head of the table. The doorbell rings.

Mrs. Castlemeyer: They are starting to show, Yvette. Do you have everything in order?

Yvette: Oui, Madame. Everything is done.

Mrs. Castlemeyer: All right, then. Go let the vultures in.

Yvette: Good evening Mr. Trust and Mr. Drysdale. Please come in and join the Madame at the table.

William Trust: You look lovely this evening, Emily. Doesn't she Melvin?

Melvin Drysdale: I agree, William. Green is my favorite color. Gold comes in a close second. She looks very alive!

Mrs. Castlemeyer: I feel like you two are sizing me up for the kill. I am very much alive and thank you for your complements. I think.

Door bell rings. Yvette lets in Dr. Feelgood and Nurse Hatchet.

Dr. Feelgood: Mrs. Castlemeyer, should you be up and around? All this excitement could wear you down.

Mrs. Castlemeyer: Doctor, you do not have to worry. I have a few things that I have to take care of tonight. We will go back to worrying tomorrow.

Nurse Hatchet: I thing she looks wonderful, Doctor. *(a little worried)* It *seems* the color is back in her face.

The Doctor and Nurse are concerned that Mrs. Castlemeyer is taking a turn for the better.

Door bell rings. Enters Monte. All of the guests moan.

Monte: Now the party can begin. I'm here. *(Slaps Mrs. Castlemeyer on her back)* Hello Emily, I'm glad I could make it tonight.

Monte tries to kiss Mrs. Castlemeyer on the lips and she turns her head and he kisses her ear.

Mrs. Castlemeyer: I'm glad you could make it also. I have a little surprise for you tonight.

Monte: *(a little concerned)* I can't wait.

Doorbell rings one last time.

Yvette: Madame, there is a lady who says she is Muffin Castlemeyer. Do I let her in?

Mrs. Castlemeyer: Yes, yes I can not believe it! Let her in Yvette.

Nurse Hatchet to the Doctor: *(Whispers)* That's not the one you hired! Who is she?

Doctor: I don't know. I've never seen her before!

Yvette wheels Mrs. Castlemeyer up to the young lady.

Mrs. Castlemeyer: Is it true what my maid has just told me? Are you my relative?

Everyone gasps. Melvin Drysdale takes out his handkerchief and wipes his brow. William Trust grabs Melvin's handkerchief and wipes his brow also.

Muffin Castlemeyer: Yes ma'am, and I can prove it to you.

Muffin pulls out a photo of her with her Uncle, Edward Castlemeyer. She also has her's and her parents' Birth Certificates.

Mrs. Castlemeyer: I am speechless. I can not believe after all of these years I have a living relative.

Muffin and Mrs. Castlemeyer hug. Everyone is upset and confused. Especially Monte.

Monte: I don't mean to interrupt, but when is dinner going to be served and what is my surprise, Emily?

Mrs. Castlemeyer: I do have a surprise for you but it concerns everyone here tonight.

William Trust: Here is the up dated Will you had me make up.

Mrs. Castlemeyer: Thank you, William. I had William rewrite my will because as many of you all ready know, I am not in good health.

Muffin: Oh no. I just found you. How can it be that you are dying?

Mrs. Castlemeyer: We will get to that in a minute, dear. Now William, I had you redo my will but late last night I had a change of heart so I wrote one myself and decided I did not want anyone to know who was receiving what. I've never been proper with money anyway!
(Looks to Melvin) Melvin, you have been a thorn in my side since I married Edward. I will never know what he saw in you. So guess what,

I'm moving my money and invest it all in Internet stock. *(someone in the back yells "Yahoo")*

Melvin Drysdale: You can't do that. I have loans I've made and besides that I have always been there for you.

Mrs. Castlemeyer: When was the last time you took me to lunch?

Melvin: Well, let me see, well that would be last, no, maybe…

Mrs. Castlemeyer: Never! I am your biggest depositor and you have never even given me a lousy lunch. You're fired!

Melvin takes out his handkerchief and begins to sob. Loudly.

Next, Dr. Feelgood and you, "trusty" Nurse. I heard what you two were cooking up yesterday. The reason the person you hired did not show was because I called and paid her off and now she is ready to testify for me if need be. Besides Nurse Hatchet you drugged my maid. Doctor and Nurse Hatchet, you are both fired. I've found me a nice young Doctor name Dr. Charles Sanders. He is checking me out tomorrow. We'll see just how sick I am.

Dr. Feelgood: I have given you the best care a Doctor could give. I will get an attorney.

William Trust: *Hands Dr. Feelgood his card and winks.* I'm your man, Doctor.

Mrs. Castlemeyer: You two go right ahead. I've had this house filled with so many recording devices I could have all of you put away for a long time!

Everyone gets quiet and starts to think.

Dr. Feelgood: Yvette, could you show me where the bathroom is?

Yvette: Oui, Oui !

Dr. Feelgood: Well, yes I have to wee wee. But you don't have to announce it!

Monte: What about me? I really do like you Emily. I may seem like a mooch but I always have a good time when we've gone out.

Mrs. Castlemeyer: If you are so interested in me as you say you are, how come my butler saw you having dinner with Nurse Hatchet last week?

Everyone gasps.

Monte: Oh that, we were just having a friendly dinner. That's all.

Mrs. Castlemeyer: Many times you have told me that you could not stand Nurse Hatchet. It seems that there is something going on that I don't know about.

Muffin: If I may interrupt, I can't believe that everyone here is after your money. Isn't there anyone that you can trust?

Mrs. Castlemeyer: As a matter of fact, there is. And that person is…

Yvette comes running into the room screaming.

Ending I

Yvette: Madam I went into the kitchen and found Dr. Feelgood dead on the floor. Someone hit him in the head with my skillet. What are we going to do? I'm so scared!

Mrs. Castlemeyer: No body move. Everyone here is a suspect. Except me of course. I have been in this room the entire night. We need to find out who has left this room, even for a minute.

Narrator: It seems that we have a problem here. How do we find out the guilty one? Yvette left the room many times. She was serving the guests. She did not do it because she is not a very strong person. She could not hit someone hard enough to kill them. There is Nurse Hatchet. She was in partnership with Dr. Feelgood. Maybe she got mad and did away with him. She couldn't have. Her and Monte were in the powder room smooching the few minutes that they were away from the others. Yuck! The next person on the list is William Trust. He is upset about being fired. He was to busy throwing a fit from losing such a profitable client and did not have time to go and kill the Doctor. What about this Muffin character? She shows up out of the blue! Come to find out she is an undercover Detective agent that Mrs. Castlemeyer hired to watch over all of the dinner guests. She has been following them for weeks now. So that leaves Melvin Drysdale. HE killed Dr. Feelgood! Turns out he was in trouble on the loan that Drysdale made for him for his new clinic, but being the shrewd business man he is, Drysdale made Feelgood buy an life insurance policy that paid the bank in the event of his death! Since Drysdale knew that he was losing Mrs. Castlemeyer he needed some quick cash so he felt he had to do away with the Good Doctor to save his own skin. Not too smart Melvin.

By the way…The only person that Mrs. Castlemeyer can trust is Yvette. She may eat raw meat and make too much tea but she is always true to her Madame.

Ending II

Muffin: If I may interrupt, I can't believe that everyone here is after your money. Isn't there anyone that you can trust?

Mrs. Castlemeyer: As a matter of fact, there is. And that person is…

Yvette comes running into the room screaming.

Yvette: Madame, I found Mr. Trust on the kitchen floor. He is not moving. I think that he is dead!

Mrs. Castlemeyer: Oh my, Muffin can you call the Police. Nobody can leave this room. Everyone is a suspect, except me of course!

Narrator: Come to find out Mr. William Trust was hit over the head with an iron skillet. Let's take the dinner guests one by one. The Banker Melvin Drysdale was pretty upset but he was also in the dining room when Mr. Trust was murdered. Mrs. Castlemeyer had just told him that she was taking all of her money out of his bank. He was too distraught to kill someone. We have Monte Cello. What a piece of work he is. He is to consumed with himself to worry about ending someone else's life. He is worried about where his next meal ticket is coming from. Then we have Dr. Feelgood, the man who has made Mrs. Castlemeyer *feel* worse. He was in the bathroom smoking a cigarette trying to calm his nerves. He had been giving Mrs. Castlemeyer a mild drug to keep her bed ridden all these weeks and is afraid she is about to find out. Actually Mrs. Castlemeyer is just plain mean, not sick! Next is Nurse Hatchet. She had Mr. Trust handle her divorce last year and was not happy with the end results. She ended up with nothing when her husband was the one who had been unfaithful! She now hated all men and decided to get rid of the one that made her life miserable. So in a fit of rage, after being fired, she hit Mr. Trust over the head in the kitchen with the iron skillet. What about Muffin? Come to find out, she is an under cover agent that Mrs. Castlemeyer hired in order to check out all of her dinner guests. She was just pretending to be a relative to Mrs. Castlemeyer.

The only person that Mrs. Castlemeyer can trust is Yvette. She may be wacky but she is always true to her Madame.

Ending III

Muffin: If I may interrupt, I can't believe that everyone here is after your money. Isn't there anyone that you can trust?

Mrs. Castlemeyer: As a matter of fact, there is. And that person is…

Yvette comes running into the room screaming.

Yvette: Madame, someone had hit Mr. Drysdale on the head. He is not moving. I'm afraid that he is dead!

Muffin: Mrs. Castlemeyer, I will call headquarters for you. Be sure no one leaves this room.

Narrator: Okay, now we have a bit of a mess here. Now why is Muffin taking charge all of a sudden? That is because Mrs. Castlemeyer hired her weeks ago to check up on all of her dinner guests. She is an under cover detective agent with the local Police force in Park Hills. Mrs. Castlemeyer was afraid that The Doctor was trying to poison her. So she had everyone checked out. The Lawyer, William Trust was in the dining room when Mr. Drysdale met his maker. He was still in shock that Mrs. Castlemeyer had the nerve to fire him. Then there was Monte. Mrs. Castlemeyer had just chastised him when Yvette ran in with the news of the murder. Nurse Hatchet was in the powder room trying to call a taxi on her cell phone. She did not want to have anything to do with the "Good" Doctor any more. That leaves the "Good" Doctor. He had left the room right before Mrs. Castlemeyer got mad at Monte. Come to find out he was also Mr. Drysdale's Doctor. Mr. Drysdale had made a pass at the Doctor's wife recently at the bank and the Doctor became insanely jealous and decided it was time to get rid of the smooth banker, so he did.

The only person that Mrs. Castlemeyer can trust is Yvette. She may be a bit wacky but she is always true to her Madame.

Mrs. Emily Castlemeyer
I could not have possibly killed anyone. I am the one everyone was after. I am such a caring person. I could never take another person life! Maybe Monte, well no, not even him.

Melvin Drysdale
I am too sophisticated to kill someone. Someone of my stature would hire a killer, not do it myself!

Monte Cello
I would not kill anybody. I'm trying to see where my next meal is coming from. Why that would take "effort" to actually kill a person.

Yvette
Me kill someone? I do not want to kill anyone. I have to go fix Madame some tea. You will talk to Madame if you have questions.

William Trust
Did you not know my last name? Trust, I am a Trust. So do not even bother to ask me again. I know my rights!

Nurse Hatchet
I am too mad at the Doctor to think about killing someone. Now I have to go out and find another job. This is not going to look good on my resume'. What am I going to do? Maybe I can get a job in a nursing home!

Dr. Feelgood
I believe that my reputation speaks for itself. I should not even have to answer that question. Kill someone, I don't think so. You want to see my diploma. I have a very important appointment now. I have to go.

Muffin Castlemeyer
Can you believe this bunch of losers? All except for Yvette and the Mrs. are about as guilty as OJ! Well, you know what I mean. Watch your backs, they cannot be trusted.

Castlemeyer Suggestions

The star of this play has got to be Yvette. She is the type who is forgetful and described as "the lights are on but no body's home"! I would have that person wear a maids costume that was wrinkled and miss buttoned. Her little hat could be crooked on her head with her hair messed up. You could go as far as to have her in one scene with shoes on that do not match. The banker and lawyer should have on suits and look very important. I would put Monte in a bright colored polyester suit with white shoes. Make him the disco guy! You could slick his hair down or even better, have him wear a bad toupe.

General Suggestions

Our group has a narrator that helps keep things running along. We have half time entertainment so that dinner can be served. We have a singing group from our church perform songs like, *Four Walls, Five Foot Two* etc. We use more country songs if the play is a western. The half time entertainment is only fifteen minutes long. At the end of the play the narrator or a different person helps the audience with the instructions on how to solve the murder. We have twelve tables of eight people. The play is performed up and down the aisle of the tables. The front and the back of the hall is where we keep our props. We charge $15.00 a person or $100.00 a table. We also have three performances. Each table is numbered. Every character goes by each table and hands out their alibi. You can have the characters hand out pencils and paper to each table so they can try and solve the case. You have three different endings so that if you want to have more than one performance you won't have the same murderer each showing. The narrator puts the time that each table's guess is handed in. That way if more than one table has the correct answer the one with the earliest time wins. He can read them all aloud if you have time. Sometimes you get some pretty wacky reasons and murderers. We have given out small gifts to the winning table like pads and pencils that have the name of our acting troop on them. You need to make this event to fit the personality of the group raising money. Make up your own system. Have fun doing it. We have a lot of fun having the characters over act or add some dialog to the play by mentioning someone local in politics or if you forget your lines, ad-lib! It's all in fun. This keeps you from selling products and doing car washes. This is a *fun* way to *fund raise*!

Food or No Food!

You may not have a place that will have access to a kitchen. Another way you can put on your play is to have a dessert play. Have ten or twelve people make their best desserts. It could be pie with ice cream and coffee and tea or maybe ice cream sundaes with all of the toppings. You can make this a *fun* way to *fund raise* to fit your groups needs and personality. So don't feel like you have to have a big dinner if it isn't possible for your group. Do what feels right for your people.

I wish you the best on your play, thanks for choosing *Hair Raisin' Funds*!

Food for thought recipes!
Please notice I put the dessert recipes first!
Dump Cake

This is a simple recipe that is really good. You can have several different people make it and have enough for 100!

1   stick of oleo or butter
1   16 oz. Can cherry pie filling
1   16 oz. Can crushed pineapple (drain)
1   yellow cake mix

Preheat your oven to 350*. Begin by layering using the pineapple on bottom of cake pan. Then add the cherry pie filling. Next top with UNCOOKED cake mix. Cut oleo or butter into small pats and lay all over the top of the uncooked cake mix. Bake for 45 minutes or until golden brown.

Chocolate Dream Pie

My husband's favorite pie

Sugar   1 ½ cups
Cocoa   ¼ cup
Pinch of salt – Mix until lumps of Cocoa are gone.
In a separate bowl mix:
Two Eggs
Evaporated milk – one 5.33 ounce can
Butter   ¼ cup-melted
Vanilla one Teaspoon (mexican if you have it)

Combine eggs, butter, milk, and vanilla in a mixing bowl; beat well. Add sugar mixture; mix well. Pour filling into pastry shell. Bake at 350 for 45 to 50 minutes. Cool before slicing. One 9 inch pie.

My Aunt Christine's Raisin Pie

Makes two pies

2   Cups white Sugar
4   Eggs
1   Stick of Butter-melted
2   Teaspoons of Vanilla
Mix the above ingredients together.
Then add the next four ingredients to the first mixture.
1 ½ Cup chopped pecans
1 ½ Cup Sun-Maid raisins
1 ½ Cup white shredded "Angel" Coconut
3   Tablespoons of vinegar

Pour into two uncooked pie shells. Bake at 325 degrees for about 45 minutes or until the pie in a little bit loose. Pie will set.

Takes about 12 to 15 minutes to mix.

Chocolate Chip Melt-A-Way

1 cup Butter (softened)	1 teaspoon baking soda
1 cup vegetable oil	1 teaspoon cream of tartar
1 cup sugar	1 teaspoon salt
1 cup powdered sugar (sifted)	1 teaspoon vanilla extract
2 eggs	1 (12 ounce) pkg. semisweet choc. Chips
4 cups all-purpose flour	Additional sugar

Combine first 5 ingredients in a large mixing bowl: beat Until smooth. Combine flour, soda, cream of tartar, and salt; Add to butter mixture. Beat until smooth; stir in vanilla and Chocolate morsels. Shape mixture into 1-inch balls; roll in Sugar. Place 2 inches apart on ungreased cookie sheets; bake At 375 degree for 10 to 12 minutes or until lightly browned. Cool cookies on wire racks. Yield: about 8 ½ dozen.

Carol S. Noble
Burgaw, North Carolina

Excellent Cookie – Makes a lot!

This one is easy and everyone loves it.

White Trash
By: Vicki George

6 Cups	*Rice Chex*
3 Cups	*Cheerios* (Can use *Malt-O-Meal*)
1 Can	Cocktail Peanuts
2 Cups	Pretzels
1 Bag	*M&M* (16 oz)
1 ½ Lbs.	White Almond Bark (1 pkg.)

Mix first five ingredients in a large roasting pan. Melt almond bark in microwave. Pour over mixture and stir. Dump on wax paper, let harden for half an hour and break up into small clumps.

This is soooo good, words can't describe it. You won't just eat one hand full. Very addictive! Can be frozen.

Lunch For 100 people

100 Baking Potatoes – Cheaper at a produce company
Grilled Ham & Cheese – 10 loaves of bread, 100 slices of cheese
                     & 100 slices of ham.
Fruit salad – two cut up large watermelons, six cantaloupes, 2 large
          Cans pineapple cubed (drained), five lb. Seedless
          Grapes & twelve apples, mix and chill.

Soup – Sam's has soup mixes that we have tried & are great. Potato and the chicken noodle are good.

Will Need:

Sour cream	Grated cheese	Bacon bits
Butter	Ice tea	Napkins
Plates	Forks	Spoons

<<<<<<<<<<<<<<<<<<<<<<<<<<<<<<<<<<<<<<<<<<<<<<<<<<<<<<<

Taco Salad

This menu is a very good way to save money

    100 Tortillas
    2 large cans pinto beans
    16 lbs. Taco meat

Lettuce	Tomatoes	Onions
Tortilla Chips	Picante Sauce	Black Olives
Sour Cream	Salad Dressings	Plates
16 oz. Cups	Napkins	Ice tea

This can be served with fruit on the side or guacamole.

Croissants

For 50 people

65 Croissants
4 ½ lbs. Thin sliced Roast Beef
3 ½ lbs. Thin sliced Turkey

Lettuce	Sliced Tomatoes	Pickles
3 Lg.bags chips	Sliced Cheese	Mayo
Mustard	Miracle Whip	Tea
Coffee	Water	Plates
Napkins	16 oz. Cups	

Can be served with fruit

<<<<<<<<<<<<<<<<<<<<<<<<<<<<<<<<<<<<<<<<<<<<<<<<<<<<<

Taquitos for 80!

15 Doz. Eggs
160 Tortillas
9 lbs. Bacon
4 – 2 lbs. Rolls of Ground Sausage (Jimmy Dean Type)
5 Bags of Hash Brown Potatoes
1 large can Refried Beans
Grated cheese
6 cans OJ
Oil
Picante Sauce

Plates   Napkins   16 oz. Cups
8 oz.cups   Bowls
Can serve with fruit.

King Ranch Chicken
For 80

200 Tortillas
12 Crm. Of Mushroom Soup
12 Crm. Of Celery Soup
Large bag of chicken breast
Bag of chicken thighs
3 Large onions
9 cans of Rotel
Grated Cheese
4 Large Bell Peppers
1 Red Bell Peppers
2 Large Corn
Lettuce
Tomatoes

Bake on 375 for an hour. Serve with corn and side salad.

<<<<<<<<<<<<<<<<<<<<<<<<<<<<<<<<<<<<<<<<<<<<<<<<<<<<<<<<<

Italian Meatballs

Four packages of meat balls-Sam's club has these. There are 26 servings per package. So four packages would be 104 servings.

18 large cans of cream of mushroom soup.

Four large packages of pasta noodles – also from *Sam's club*.

When you heat up meatballs add soup and you can add milk or water to make the gravy more creamy. Cook the noodles according to the instructions on the package.

Green Beans – 4 large cans
Serve with a side salad.

We tried this with rice. The rice had to be cook in small boilers and it took longer than the noodles. We got more complements on this meal than any other.

Crab and Shrimp Dip

*Put **two 1/3 less fat cream cheese** in heavy boiler on medium to medium low heat.. Add **cream of chicken soup**. Chop up ½ **cup of celery** and ½ **cup green onions** and add to mixture. Add **1 teaspoon of Worcester** sauce and **1 teaspoon of Tabasco** to mixture. When mixture is creamy add **1 can of white crab meat** and **1 can of tiny shrimp (drain both crab & shrimp)**. When the dip is bubbling and smooth put **3 tablespoons of cold water** in a bowl with a **small packet of unflavored Knox gelatin**. Pour gelatin into mixture and stir well. Pour dip into a Jell-O mold container and refrigerate for at least eight hours.*

This dip goes a very long way. Could be used for a group of 25.

<<<<<<<<<<<<<<<<<<<<<<<<<<<<<<<<<<<<<<<<<<<<<<<

Cheese Ball

2   *8 oz. 1/3 less fat crème cheese*
1   *pkg. Smoked ham lunch meat, chopped (69cent kind!)*
½   *bundle of green onion, chopped*
     Chopped pecans
     Tabasco to taste

Mix crème cheese, ham, onion and about 1/3 of a cup of chopped nuts in a bowl. Add Tabasco. Shape into a ball and pat chopped pecans on ball until completely coated. Serve with chips and snack crackers. Best if it sits in the frig for a few hours.

Samples of forms

<table>
<tr>
<td>

The 2003
W. A. A. T.
(Wesley's Amateur Actors Troupe)

hopes you enjoyed tonight's production of

"INCIDENT AT THE ROAD KILL CAFÉ"

Would you like advance information on
Future shows? If so, please complete the
Following information so we may add you
To our mailing list.

Name:_____

Address:_____

#:_____ City:_____

Zip Code:_____

See Ya Next Year!

</td>
<td>

Solution Form

TIME:_____

TABLE NUMBER:_____

WHO DONE IT?_____

_____

_____

The 2003 W.A.A.T.
(Wesley's Amateur Actors Troupe)

hopes you enjoyed tonight's production

Of: "Incident At The Road Kill Café"

See ya next Year!

</td>
</tr>
</table>

We put several of these forms on each table. It has brought us a whole bunch of repeat business.

Suzann Carr

About the Author

Suzann Carr is a playwright; active in W.A.A.T.S. (Wesley Amateur Actors Troupe) she also works with her husband at their insurance agency. She has been involved with fund raising for her church, her son's elementary school, her daughter's band and the youth group at church. She lives in Corpus Christi, Texas with her husband and their two children. Suzann is currently working on her sixth play. *Udder Nonsense*!